KRUECK ■ SEXTON

FROM THERE TO HERE

With an introduction
by John Morris Dixon

images
Publishing

Contents

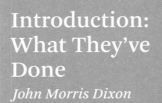

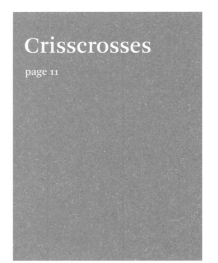
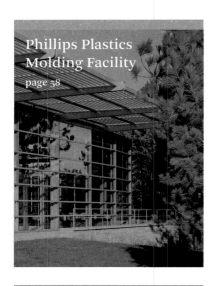
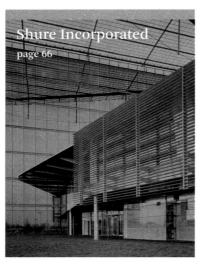

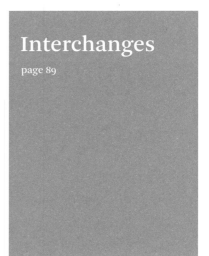
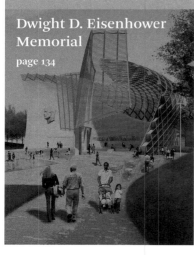
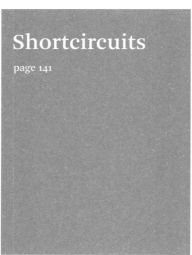
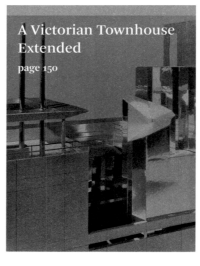
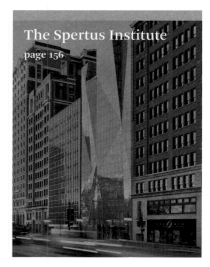

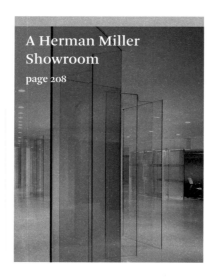
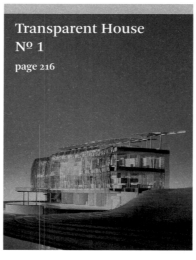

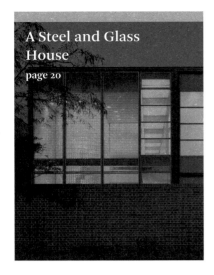
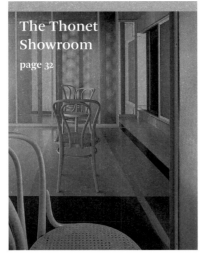

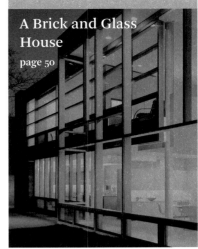

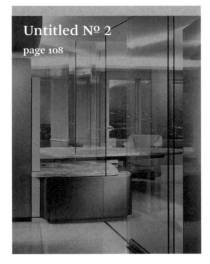

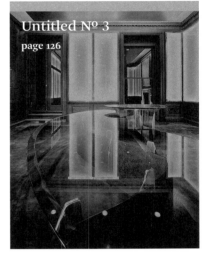

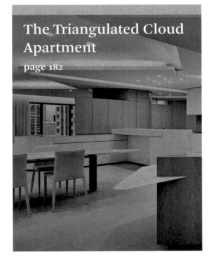
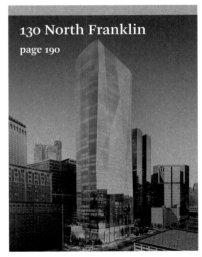

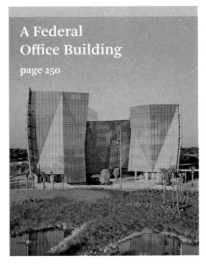
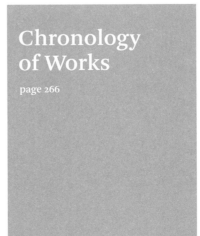

Introduction: What They've Done

John Morris Dixon

I'VE BEEN ADMIRING Krueck + Sexton's accomplishments since 1981, when the firm's superb Steel and Glass House claimed our attention at *Progressive Architecture* magazine. It was their very first work, yet it was an incredibly mature one, impeccably carried out to the smallest detail—and a herald of things to come. We featured it as our cover story in the December issue that year. Ron Krueck is quoted there as likening the house to taking the pioneering modernist Mies van der Rohe's "simple sentences" and using his vocabulary to "make complex sentences and paragraphs."

Throughout the middle decades of the twentieth century, Mies was revered among architects for the purity of his design, especially in his adopted city of Chicago. But by the early 1980s, at the time of that seminal house, much of the architecture profession was in rebellion against the constraints of modernism. No longer hoping to totally replace the inherited built fabric, architects acknowledged that their work would have to fit into existing contexts. They began looking at historical architecture with renewed respect. And even in that bastion of modernism, Chicago, postmodern allusions to hitherto scorned historical styles were beginning to appear in new buildings.

While Krueck and partner Mark Sexton understood the need to adapt modernism to its updated role in our built environment, they did not respond with design quotations from the past. Nor did they, like some of their fellow late modernists, employ new forms for their own sake or simply to exploit evolving technology. Both of them are alumni of the architecture program Mies established at the Illinois Institute of Technology in 1939, where architecture students were infused with the fundamentals, rigors, and self-criticism set forth there. Liberating themselves from this program, they looked to early modernism for its deeper lessons about design.

The architects credit their student experience with developing their fine judgment of proportion—the dimensional relationships within and between the elements of buildings. Meticulously calibrated proportions, scales, and space were intensely stressed at IIT. One reason the firm's work is so elegant—so unassailably right—is that the proportions are studied meticulously while at the same time a seamless integration of space, structure, and materials is established. The partners also credit collage exercises at IIT with developing their skills at composing overlapping planes and volumes, which contribute so crucially to the visual and spatial richness of their works. Krueck stayed on at IIT as a studio professor for thirty years.

Krueck and Sexton cite, as well, influences from beyond their immediate experiences, such as the writings of architectural theorist Colin Rowe and the visionary proposals of architect John Hejduk. From the art world, they have been inspired by the "spaceless space" in the paintings of Barnett Newman, the hard-edged shapes and vivid colors of Ellsworth Kelly, and the works of Agnes Martin, which reveal subtle differences among repetitive units, compared by Sexton to the variations among leaves on a tree.

Krueck sees precedents for the expansion of their design vocabulary beyond the rectangle in the art of Frank Stella, who created assemblages of vividly colored angular and curved shapes in which the spaces between count as much as the solids. And he recalls finding inspiration for the firm's compositions in a fluid painting of a diamond ring rendered in comic-strip style by Roy Lichtenstein—calling this work a "baroque Mondrian."

Yet external influences cannot fully account for what these architects have achieved. Their distinctive visual explorations in three dimensions are strictly their own. They have learned the most from what Sexton calls "the art of making"—the orchestration of the innumerable elements that compose a work of architecture. "We learn from what we've done," Krueck emphasizes. The Chicago architecture critic Blair Kamin observed over a decade ago that Krueck and Sexton function as "a true partnership, relying on their complementary talents. Krueck conceptualizes. Sexton questions. Krueck refines."

Salient aspects of Krueck + Sexton's works include an unusual awareness of the effects of light—the architects control it as a design element. Starting in that first house, they have consciously generated spatial configurations that differ when perceived under varying light conditions—by day or night. In more recent projects, they have made highly effective use of screens and reflections to maximize natural lighting and minimize heat gain.

The firm also has shown an unprecedented and masterful handling of color, texture, finish, and translucency. Particularly notable in some of their works is the use of spatial stratagems, which they call "veils of transparency"—most vividly in their Painted Apartment and Thonet Showroom. Veiling devices include perforated metal and glass with subtly adjusted degrees of transparency—clear, tinted, frosted, sandblasted, fritted, and in the form of glass block. They have also played skillfully with the varying degrees of reflection off of clear glass set at different angles.

Early in their practice, the partners realized that existing modernist furniture, however elegant, did not always fit comfortably into their interiors. For several projects, they designed their own chairs and tables—usually more boldly sculptural than familiar classics and typically conceived as components of the total design. In many cases, built-in cabinetry and seating are integral to the shaping of spaces.

While Krueck + Sexton's early commissions were mostly limited to houses, apartments, and commercial interiors, the firm has moved on to works in a wide range of types and scales. Their portfolio now includes substantial office and institutional buildings, skyscrapers, and that unclassifiable civic-scale contribution to Chicago, the Crown Fountain.

In discussing their projects, the partners reflect thoughtfully on the inevitable impact of programs and sites. But they especially highlight the roles of their clients. Any client commissioning Krueck + Sexton is naturally aiming for design distinction. The partners, accordingly, speak of their works as collaborations with discerning clients. They recall with particular satisfaction the concern shown by the owners of the workplaces documented in this book for the daylight and views enjoyed by all occupants—and those clients' willingness to invest in architectural quality.

The partners consider their achievements since that first house in 1981 as a process of evolution. It has likewise been an evolution in the geometries they have made their own. This sequence of geometrical explorations is the basis for the structure of this book. And every step in the sequence confirms Krueck + Sexton's transformation of the spare modernist tradition the partners emerged from into the expressive architecture so eloquently documented on the following pages.

A Story Told

Ron Krueck

*The world knows only a beautiful work itself and not
its origins, the conditions under which it comes into
being, for if people had knowledge of the sources
from which the artist derives his inspiration they
would oftentimes be confused and alarmed and thus
vitiate the effects the artist had achieved.*

—Thomas Mann, 1912

AT THE START OF OUR architectural studies, each
of us first focused on the point of a pencil, slowly
coming to understand what kind of line would be
produced. That understanding defines the edges
of our work today; it was also the beginning of our
examination of planes, curves, and the "spaceless
space" of a sheet of paper, which would eventually
energize our manipulation of abstract relationships.
In truth, it was the launching of a voyage that would
generate the foundations of our work.

We feel that in nature, there are truths that we
must find to reflect what cannot be seen. One of
these is that nature does not duplicate itself, though
it is in a process of continually evolving and refining.
Each of our projects is an evolution of our ideas and
intuitions and an exploration of the experiences
and freedoms that were liberated in the preceding
projects. These evolutions, one after another,
allowed us to go places we had not known before.
Each advance established new spheres, places that
our rigorous education had previously prohibited
us from going. Upon reflection, these developments

appear premeditated and direct, though that was never our intent. We were not interested in perfecting a system; we were interested in what our new freedoms made possible. This continuous course is reminiscent of the investigations of what is absent and what is present in the accomplishments of European modernists like Behrens, Le Corbusier, Loos, and Mies.

For us, intuition is not static: it is persistent. Though it might have been intuition that allowed us to make the first marks with that pencil, it was also intuition that would not let us rest until our work was brought into resolution. At times, intuition would demand that we erode or break a carefully constructed solution, perhaps exposing unforeseen potentials, which would in turn require that the freed components be rechoreographed.

The path of our work was furthered by the making of our work. Making established another understanding—of the connections, of the space required between the parts, and of the delineation of appropriate edges that would create a continuous movement. It was fundamental that materials be what they wanted to be and that details be infused with the aesthetics of the whole. The art of making reinforces the integrity of our work and positions it to simultaneously reflect the technology of the moment and endure the test of time. At every point of the design process, numerous professional voices—filtered by the architects in our studio—introduce even more innovative criteria, which continue to ground our intuition.

The words in this book are what we see and understand today. They are not the deliberate thoughts we had as we carved out the designs. It is through perspective lenses that we can analyze and review our work. This analysis has led us to the four sections of this book, each of which reflects a fundamental force that instigated specific solutions. The internal dynamics that occurred in the development and eventual integration of rectangles, curves, and facets are reflected in the section titles Crisscrosses, Interchanges, Shortcircuits, and Combines.

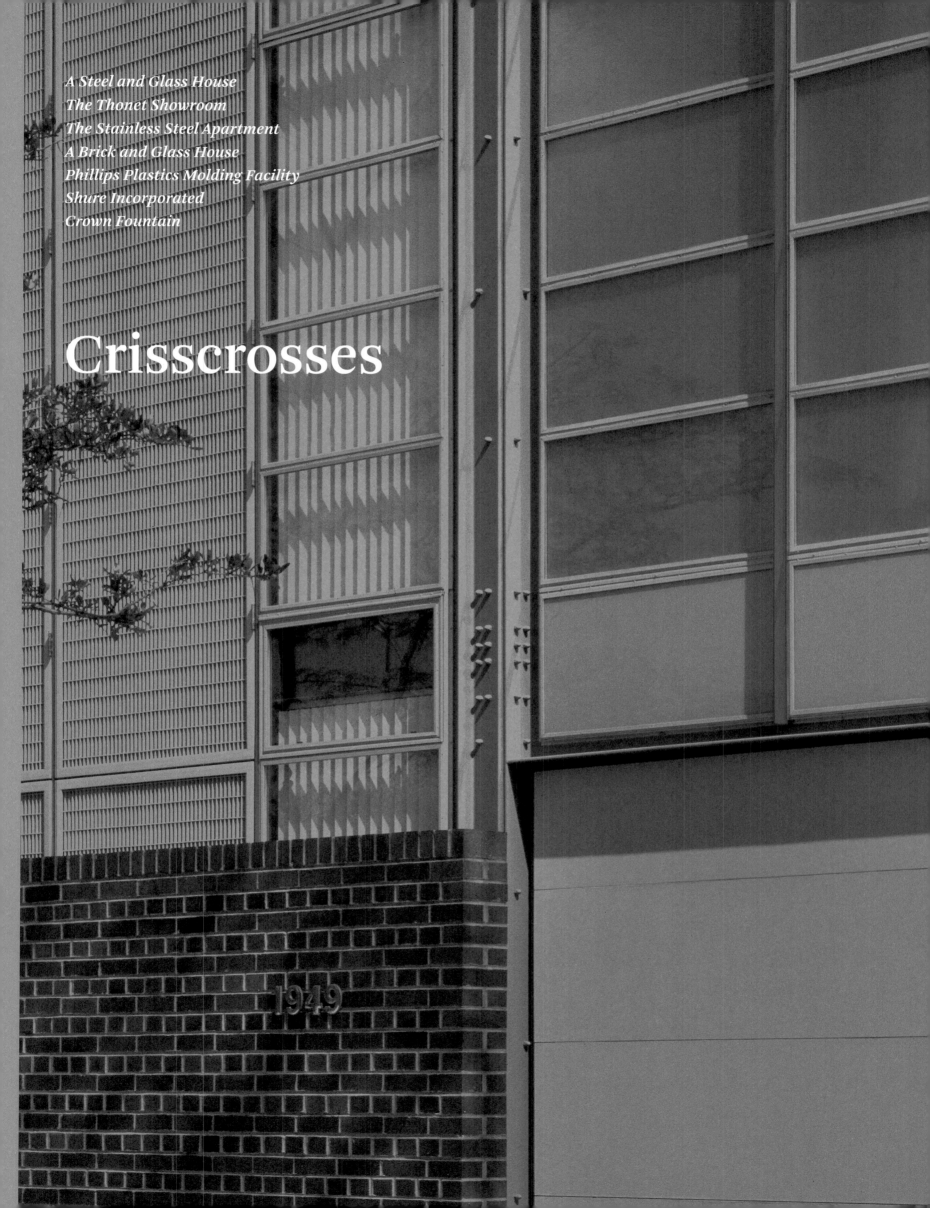

Crisscrosses

WE TYPICALLY START a project by drawing a rectangle on a sheet of paper. We delineate what is within this rectangle and also focus on the imaginary space it defines. But what is most interesting is what is outside the rectangle: the edges need to dissolve to incorporate the spaces beyond. Our moves of the pencil across the infinite grid of the paper, indicating structure and possible planning modules, begin to be clarified and annotated as the grid takes on scale. As elevations and sections are generated, which modulate and integrate the facades and spaces of the building, we picture the space of the rectangle magically unfolding out of the paper.

Our first project was sculpted by means of exactly this system. As we worked on what would become A Steel and Glass House, we saw that a U-shaped plan, around a courtyard, would provide a private outdoor space and ample daylight on the urban site. But a U shape was too baroque for us; the rectangle was sacred, so we decided to sever the U into three rectangles.

That initial breach was reinforced by rotating the structural systems of the two arms of the U. Because of that, Mies's classic inverted corner detail appears not at a corner but at the three-fifths point on the front facade, where the two systems shear. The slice between the primary rectangle and the arms is a reveal of light, a series of clear windows that runs up the front facade, across the roof as a continuous skylight, and down the rear wall as a second vertical series of windows.

Apparent in A Steel and Glass House, and indeed in many of our projects, is an acknowledgment of the dominant urban grid that characterizes Chicago. In this first residence, masonry garden walls frame the property, align with the facades of neighboring houses, and define an entry court. The walls identify and protect the property's limits. Inside the house, rectangular planes and volumes overlap and intersect in multilayered compositions. At the time of this house, we didn't appreciate that the steps we took would be so liberating. The freedoms we exposed within the allegedly rigid language of rectangles opened our eyes to new perspectives and made possible all that has followed.

The garden walls of A Brick and Glass House accentuate the isolated residence behind them as they perceptually extend the house beyond its actual envelope and tie it into the community—into the geometry of the neighborhood and the greater grid of the city. The interior spaces are compositions of volumes and planes that appear to be suspended within the rectilinear space. A mural in the living area concentrates and amplifies the energies in these assemblages.

The Stainless Steel Apartment is the only duplex in Mies's celebrated 860–880 Lake Shore Drive buildings. The stainless steel employed for all insertions within the apartment—whether ribbed, fluted and painted, brushed, welded and burnished—contrasts with Mies's more disciplined, direct use of factory steel. We carved an elongated cut between the two floors to both open and unite them. This opening centralized the space and released the vertical compression in the apartment. Along with an obligation to our clients—to fit specific accommodations within the given volume—we wanted once again to push the space of the apartment beyond the grid of its window wall, to extend it out into the city instead of keeping it locked inside. With these disruptions, our composition of rectangles linked the interior to the city beyond the planes of glass, restoring the distinctive visual qualities of the scene outside to the space inside.

If the houses and the apartment are a universal dialogue with the rectangle, The Thonet Showroom—which we subtitled "Homage to Barnett Newman | Homage to El Lissitzky"—is a study of the nucleus of that rigor. Here, all interaction among rectangles is confined to eight vertical feet between two unforgiving planes: floor and ceiling. We inserted translucent and perforated metal screens; painted projections of the colors of the frames' edges release and delineate the energies of the screens. The spaceless space of the floors, ceilings, and walls is modulated by this free grid of projected lines, which establishes interlocking phenomenal rectangles of different densities. Specific hues of gray paint reinforce these densities. The multiple readings of the space are recalibrated by rows of vertical fluorescent tubes that cast light of different color temperatures. Denying weight, these carefully produced phenomenal transparencies create a sense of suspension within a multifaceted world. Entering this space is like walking into a gemstone.

For two exurban industrial projects, Phillips Plastics Molding Facility and Shure Incorporated, we extended and elaborated on rectangular "found objects." At Phillips, the foundations for the main manufacturing volume had been poured before we were hired. We assimilated the horizontal plane into a larger composition of rectangular configurations, even though the boundaries and contours of the unspoiled site were not at all rectangular. The building we designed is a series of moves that initiates a scale responsive to, and dispersed by, the existing forces. The actual factory—the molding facility—is a high-bay volume, and we added rectangular planes, horizontal and vertical, to break down the scale and singleness of the mass. The planes slide past each other, overcoming the singularity of an otherwise hierarchical box. Simple planar manipulations, such as extending the sunscreen to integrate the components both within the building and within the landscape, helped to change a simple building into an elevated workplace.

At Shure, a prominent manufacturer of microphones, we added a research center to a multistory office building, our found rectangular object. The client wanted to minimize the distinction between two groups of employees: those who work in offices and those who work in labs. We created shared spaces, but more important, we devised a single new entrance between the old and the new buildings that offers to all a broad, welcoming, transparent lobby.

Rectangular planes extending from the structure project the energy of the workplace beyond the glass facade. An exterior screen floats outside the line of the building; because of its visual delicacy and transparency, it visibly fluctuates as it reaches out to embrace the surrounding space. Below the screen, we pulled the ground floor back to amplify the projection and break down the unity of the volume. A hundred-foot-long display exhibiting Shure's eighty-year dedication to excellence conceptually and physically links the atriums of both volumes, further integrating the original office building with the new research center. A precisely tuned theater, carved out within the original office building, demonstrates Shure equipment at its highest levels of performance.

Our objective for the Crown Fountain was apparent simplicity, and at first glance the work appears uncomplicated. However, this is a deceptive simplicity, one that required rigorous detailing. When we took on the commission, no one could figure out how to build artist Jaume Plensa's vision: a pair of glass towers with continuous shells of hand-made glass block that held twenty-two-by-forty-nine-foot LED screens behind a waterfall. Plensa had become frustrated by the challenges and was willing to accept columns or other visible supports holding up the translucent towers. Keeping true to the clarity of his original concept, we created instead a hidden egg-crate frame tied back into a deeper structure. The glass volumes are pure in form only because of their hidden complexity.

The most surprising outcome at the Crown Fountain is the activation of the space between the fountain's towers. It was envisioned as a quiet place to walk through, or to sit in and observe the art. But it became a magical room, an amphitheater for gathering, for people watching, for play. Whether serene or loud and energetic with splashing kids, it is a transportive and transformative space.

Even though we have explored a variety of geometries in our work, we have not lost our fascination with the potentials of the rectangle. When used to dissolve space, to extend active participation from one place to the place beyond, and to expose the unconventional prospects of materiality, it is the foundation of our practice and continues to be the basis for some of our most gratifying works.

A Steel and Glass House

Chicago, Illinois, 1981

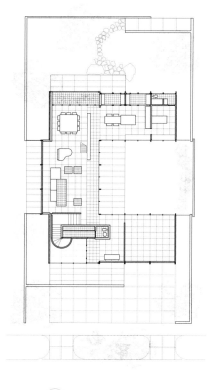

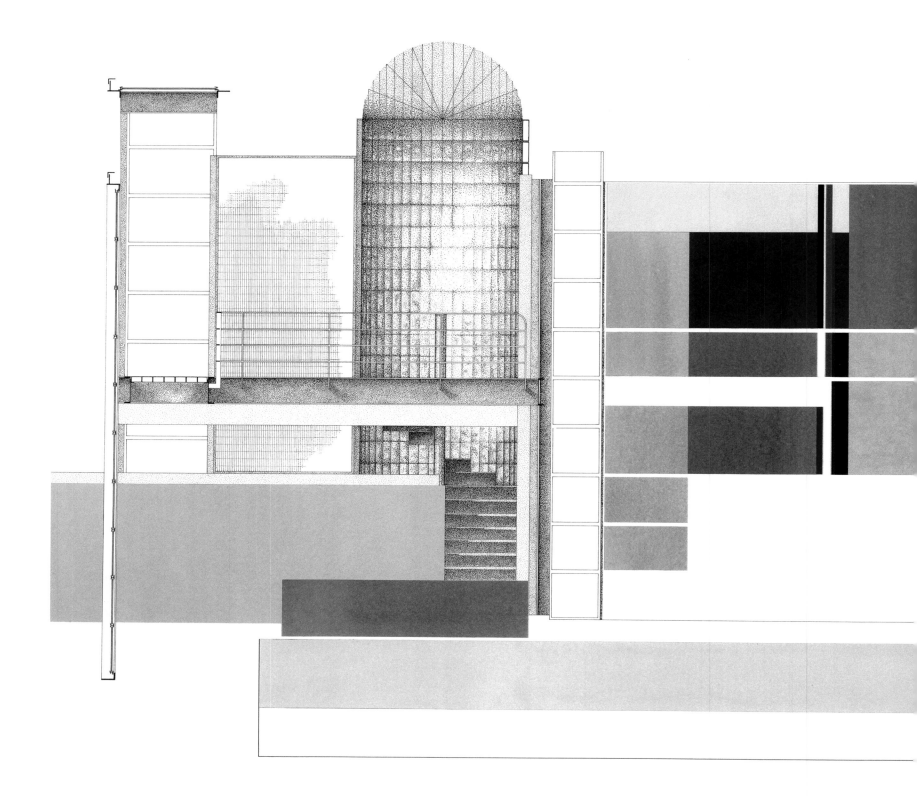

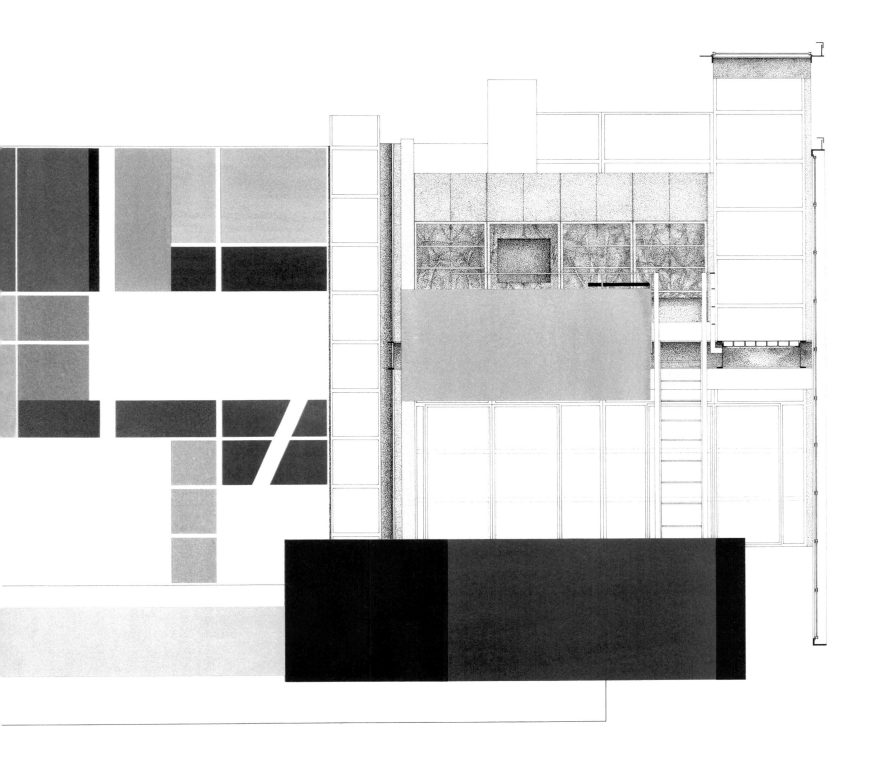

The Thonet Showroom

Chicago, Illinois, 1982

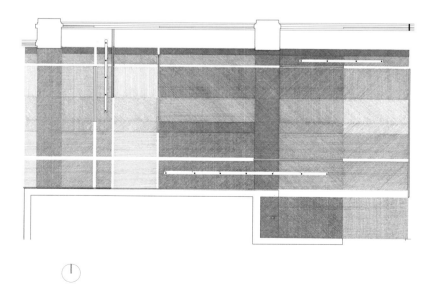

HOMAGETOBARNETTNEWMAN

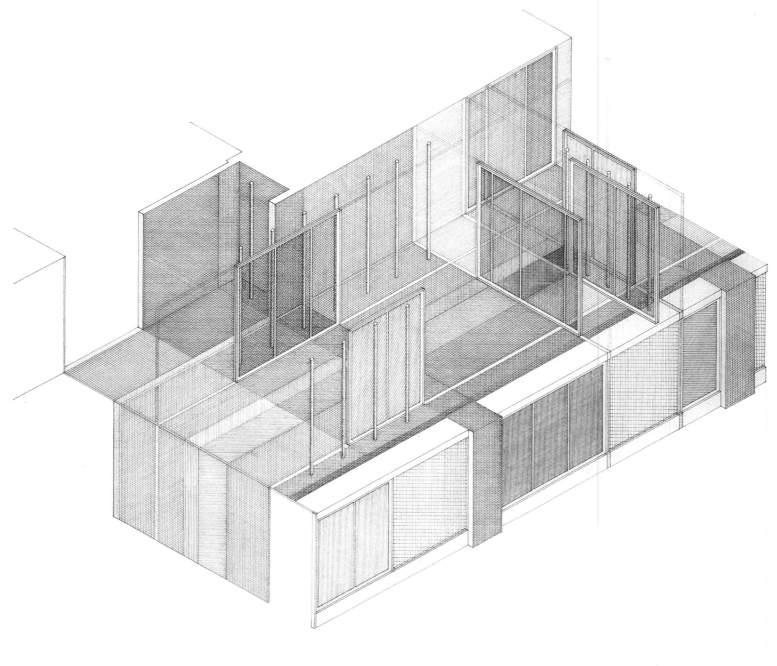

HOMAGETOELLISSITZKY.

T H O N E T

The Stainless Steel Apartment

Chicago, Illinois, 1992

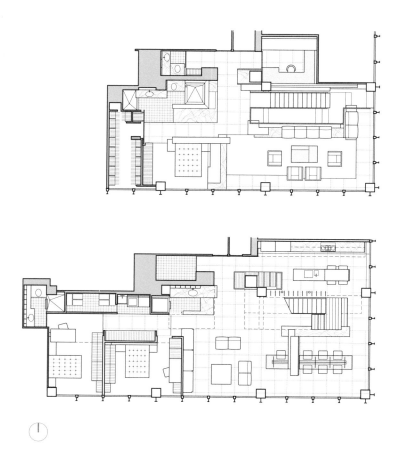

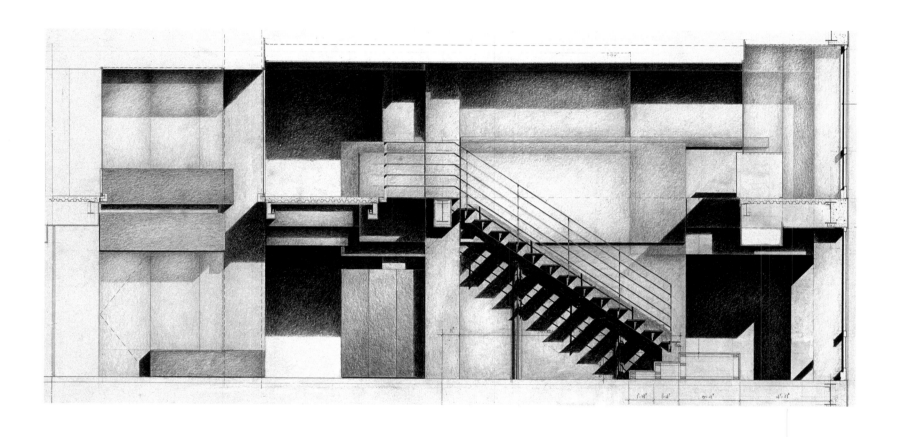

A Brick and Glass House

Chicago, Illinois, 1996

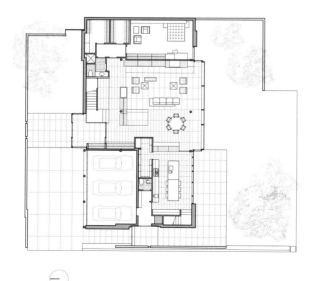

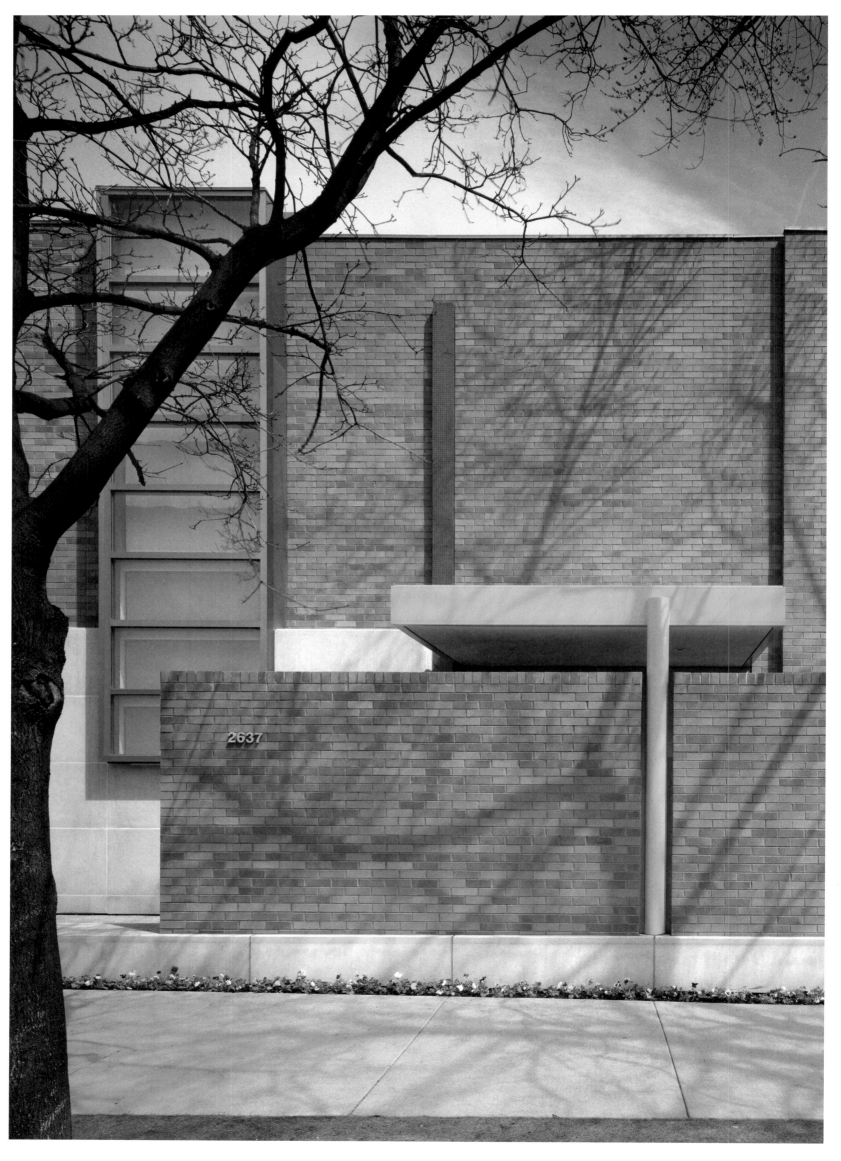

Phillips Plastics Molding Facility

Phillips, Wisconsin, 2001

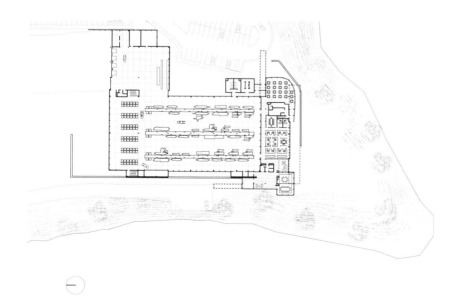

PHILLIPS PLASTICS MOLDING FACILITY 63

Shure Incorporated

Niles, Illinois, 2004–2016

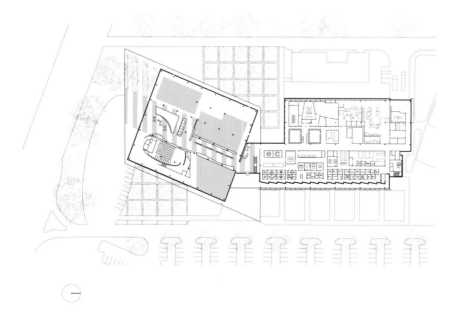

We are in business to perform a Service to people. "People" includes our customers, our employees, our suppliers, and the communities in which we live.

S.N. Shure

Crown Fountain

Chicago, Illinois, 2004

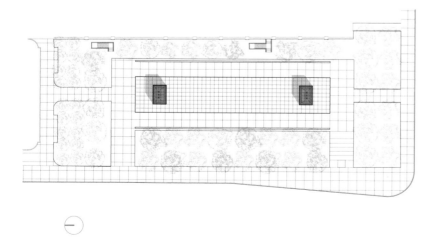

Interchanges

THE CURVE INTRIGUES us in its acceptance of different pressures; it establishes an implied continuity. While the curve is not inherently freer than the rectangle, it is more reflective of nature, since no pure rectangles exist in the organic world. Often growing out of efforts to accommodate functions within limits, the curve introduces another way to shape form and space and to express function, movement, and speed.

Even for projects that are dependent on the curve, our design explorations start with the rectangle—with program demands represented by rectangles, and with rectangular spaces in which we must work. That was true of The Painted Apartment. The setting was one of Mies's rigorously gridded apartment buildings, and we began our work with no thought of curves. The client stated, simply, that she didn't want to hang paintings, she wanted to live in a painting. She had seen The Thonet Showroom, where we had created a painterly world, so the request was a natural one. But we did not yet understand how to accommodate real-world functions within this type of other-worldly environment.

Areas for living and dining competed with circulation for the same spaces. We realized that allowing all parts to be what they wanted to be would produce curved planes instead of rectangular partitions. As these curves became central to the composition, they began to oscillate, and the primary curve was broken into three parts: one to define the dining area, where a round table would fix a center; one to extend circulation and the living area; and one to mediate the discrepancies between the first two. None of the curved spaces exists in isolation; each is experienced in relation to its opposite.

The curved dividers in The Painted Apartment are not opaque but are composed of clear glass, backlit glass block, and metal-framed perforated screens. The colors of the screens are extended in paint onto the floors and ceilings. The attraction to the opposing space is so strong that it eroded the surfaces of the screens. The dividers and the stenciled dots represent the dissipation of forces; their extensions always meet the edges of the rectangular apartment perpendicularly.

The screens constitute a focus rather than an edge, altering perception of the density of light, the reflectivity of materials, and the color of space. As light conditions change, and the occupants go about their daily routines, the spatial readings are continuously transformed in a way that recalls Laszlo Moholy-Nagy's *Light-Space Modulator*. The true delight of what we designed wasn't evident until it was realized.

Circulation also prompted the introduction of curves into the Untitled Nº 1 and Untitled Nº 2 apartments, where they helped us work through the complications of arranging effective spaces between the structural columns and mediating the restrictions of mechanical risers. Less conventional arcs with abruptly shifting radii were calibrated to the dimensions of the apartments. The shifting radii gave rise to elongated curves with blunted corners and gently expanding sides that seem to respond to some internal force. The form appears in the two apartments in the positioning of partitions, the modulation of ceiling levels and floors, and the design of furnishings.

In Untitled Nº 2, we conceived the plan spatially, as clusters of objects. To retain the freedoms and delicacies of our sketches, we made the curvilinear objects appear to float between the planes of floor and ceiling. Each form was first isolated—wrapped in a surface of distinctive color and reflectivity—and then united by extended curved ceiling planes of different heights. These curved planes are essential to the apartment's composition, compressing its space toward the building exterior. In fact, to accentuate the difference between the space and the world beyond, we lined the enclosure with a vertical plane. Its apertures, smaller than those of the original glazing, deny the reality of its framing.

Every aspect of the design defers to the geometry, resulting in a holistic environment.

A similar approach to detailing and color characterizes Untitled Nº 1. Swift, long curves of glass simultaneously separate and integrate a central double-height atrium and the more conventional living spaces of the apartment. We inserted a bridge—a glass walkway—to connect the apartment's second level on either side of the atrium space. The geometry of the bridge corresponds in plan to the reflecting pool below it, initiating a dialogue between levels. A skylight that extends to the curved edges of the atrium affirms the integration on and between levels. The stair that links the glass bridge to the main level is enclosed by glass facets that appear to have been shattered by the strong forms of the dominant glass curves. These facets sharply distinguish the stair from the curved elements and simultaneously alter its transparency. Untitled Nº 2 and Untitled Nº 1 share similar finishes. However, in Untitled Nº 1, eighteen different granites and marbles establish the grounding components. Their innate weight and patterns are juxtaposed to the metallic automotive paints and upholstered surfaces used elsewhere in the apartment.

In Untitled Nº 3, the curves respond to a very different set of circumstances. The apartment occupies the piano nobile of the McCormick

Mansion, designed by Stanford White in 1891. Our client was intrigued by the grand rooms and historic detailing, but at heart she was a minimalist, and her favorite color was black. In an inversion of the usual approach, we created a dialogue that reinforced the perimeters of the rooms as the foreground and our insertions as the background. We used curves to ease transitions, reestablish axes, and soften the impact of new partitions, screens, cabinetry, and furniture. The additions distinguish themselves from the rectilinear setting, yet their careful proportions, natural materials, and saturated colors reinvigorate the unique historic context. The relationship between foreground and background corresponds to that between symmetry and asymmetry. Symmetry prevails at the entrance and in the more formally laid out living spaces; in the more private areas, asymmetry dominates. The progression from the relatively minimal interventions in the historic rooms to the futuristic and fractured surfaces of the bedroom—a curve through time—reinforces these associations.

The competition design for the Dwight D. Eisenhower Memorial develops the curve at a civic scale. The rectangular site, a block of exterior space that had to be integrated into the municipal fabric, was divided into two triangles by a diagonal axis radiating from the Capitol. We placed the memorial and a reflecting pool on one side of the diagonal and a peace park on the other. The forces inherent in the site, along with the need to provide shelter, required curves in the third dimension. This initiated the integration of the two halves; this integration, in turn, helped to resolve the conflicts between the city's grid and its diagonal avenues.

The principal structure we proposed for the memorial was an eroded shell of multiple curvatures, an extension of the ground plane. It was a civic interpretation of the front porch, which was prominent in a historic photograph of General Eisenhower at his boyhood home in Kansas. Slightly elevated above the ground, the typical American front porch is a personal space and a community space. Our shell is in effect a porch at an urban scale; it sits on a raised stone platform, and it both enfolds a dedicated space and allows this space to merge into its surroundings. We chose white marble, the capital city's characteristic material, to give the memorial a strength and continuity that suit both the city and the commemorative intent. Reverberations of the curved stone shell extend into the landscape, molding berms that define the pool and park areas while establishing acoustic and visual separation from the surrounding streets. The design of the front porch and the peace park reflects Eisenhower the individual, the general, and the president, and would have been a place of tribute that brought people together.

The Painted Apartment

Chicago, Illinois, 1983

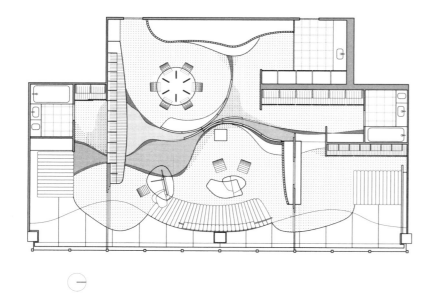

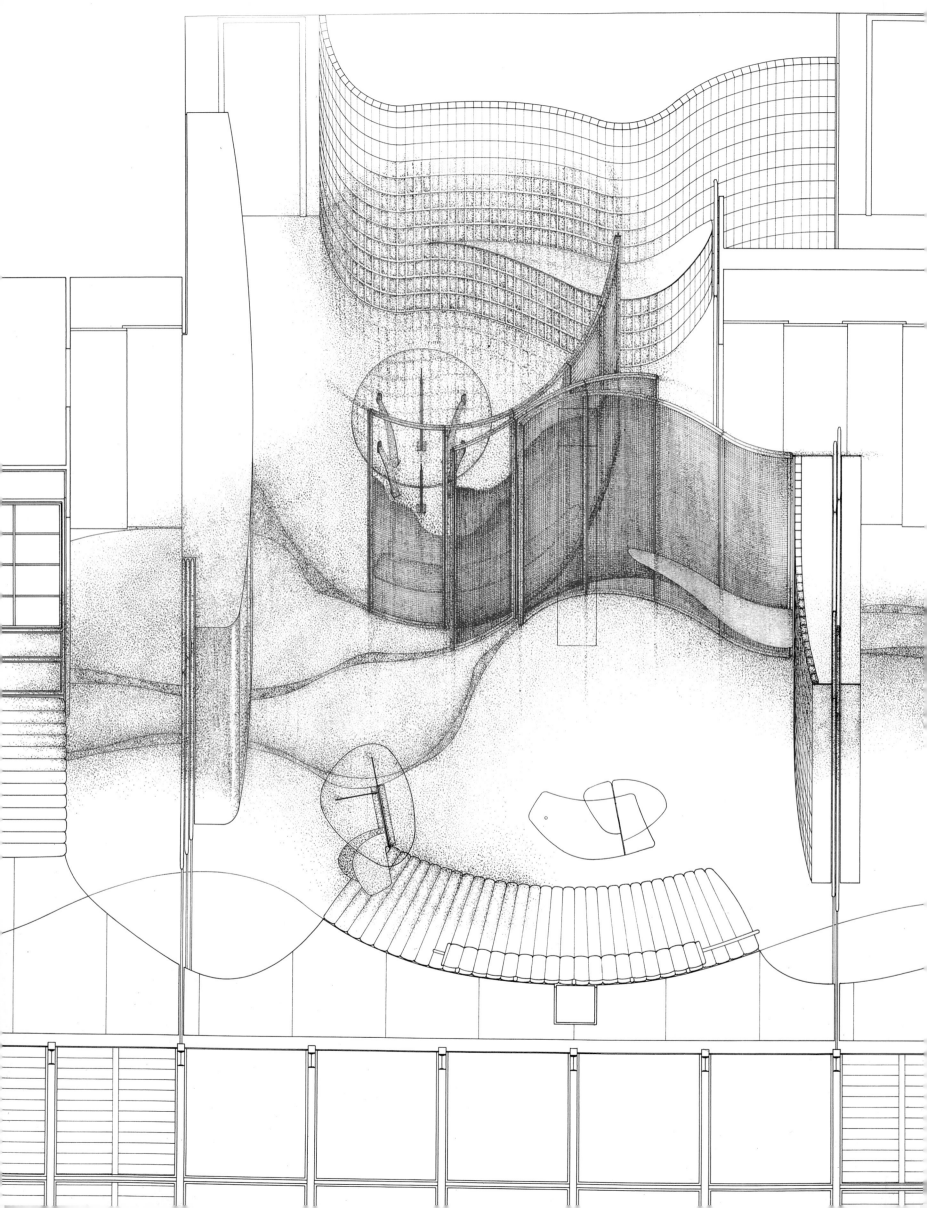

Untitled № 2

Chicago, Illinois, 1988

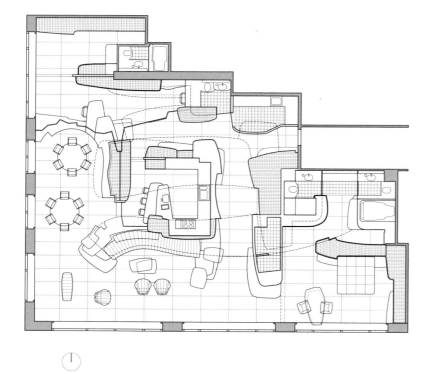

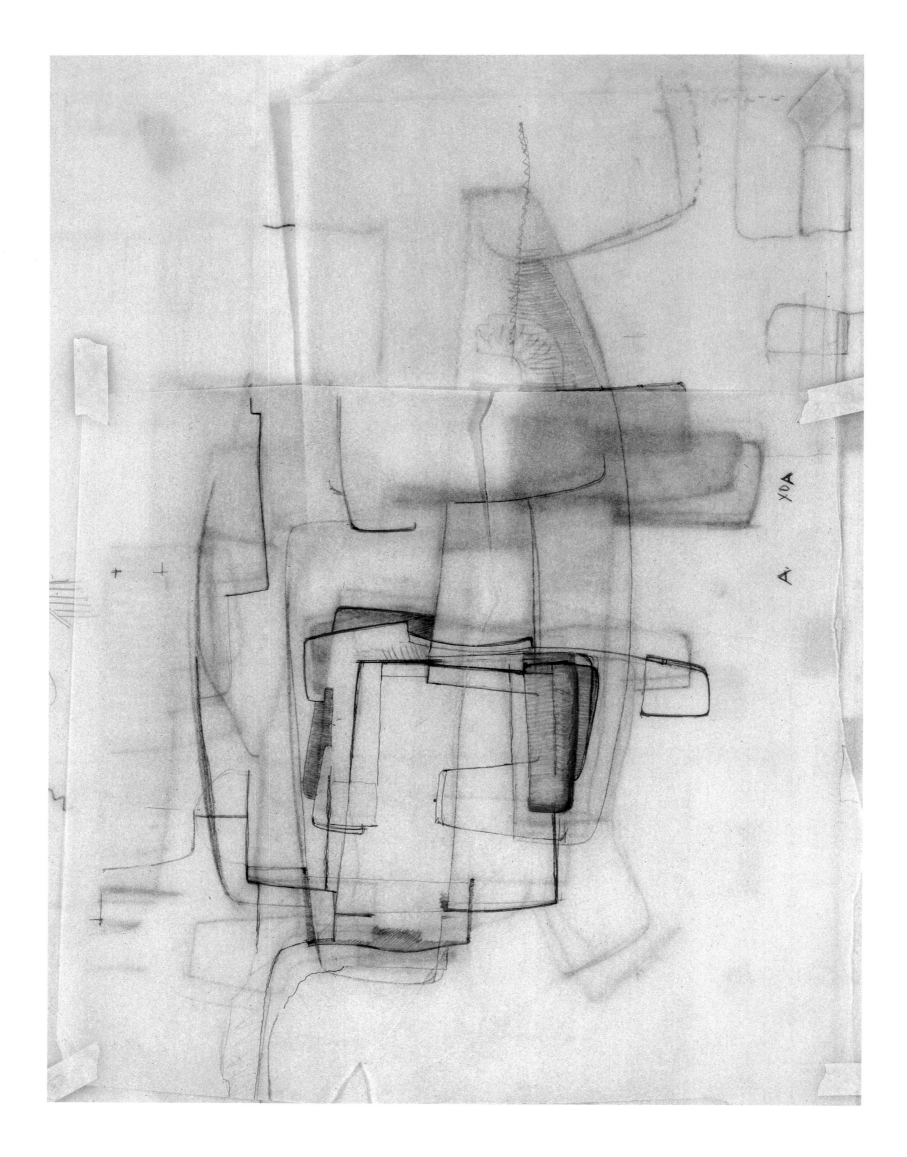

Untitled № 1

Chicago, Illinois, 1987

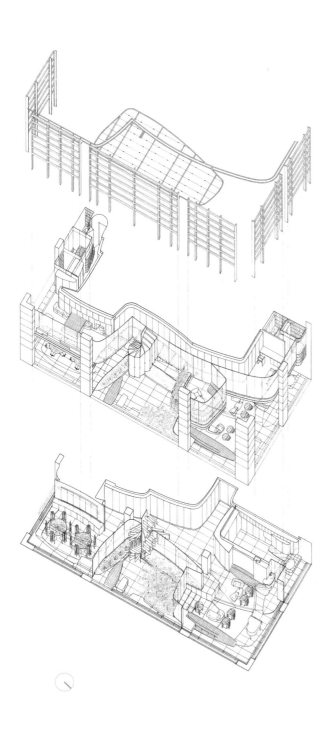

Untitled № 3

Chicago, Illinois, 1986

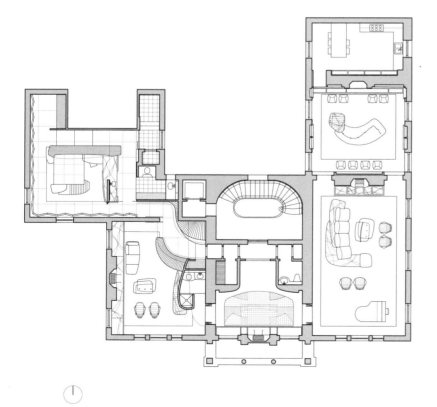

Dwight D. Eisenhower Memorial

Washington, DC, 2009

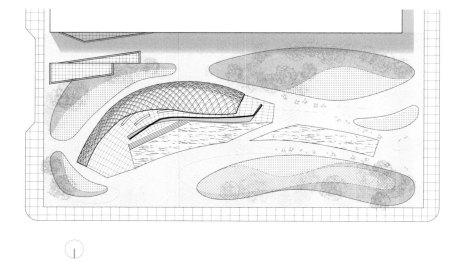

DWIGHT D. EISENHOWER NATIONAL ME

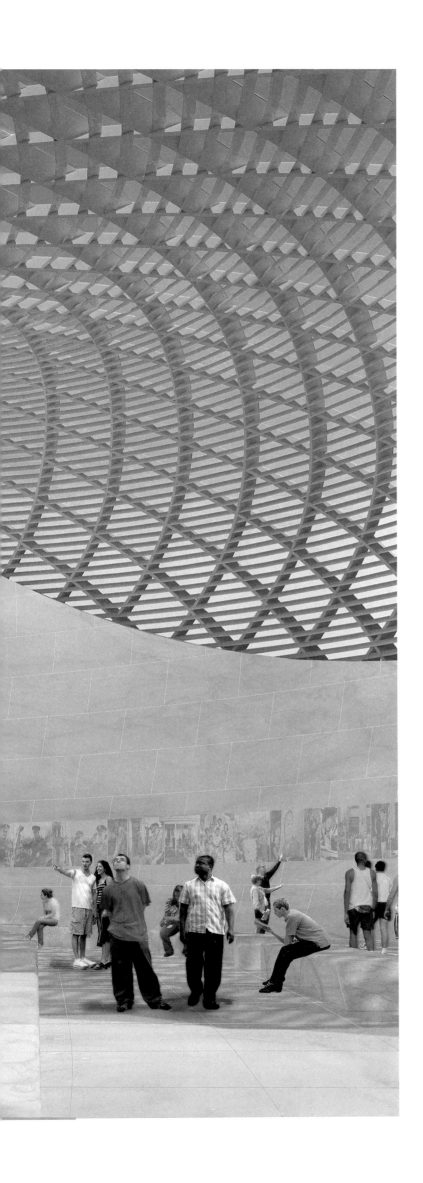

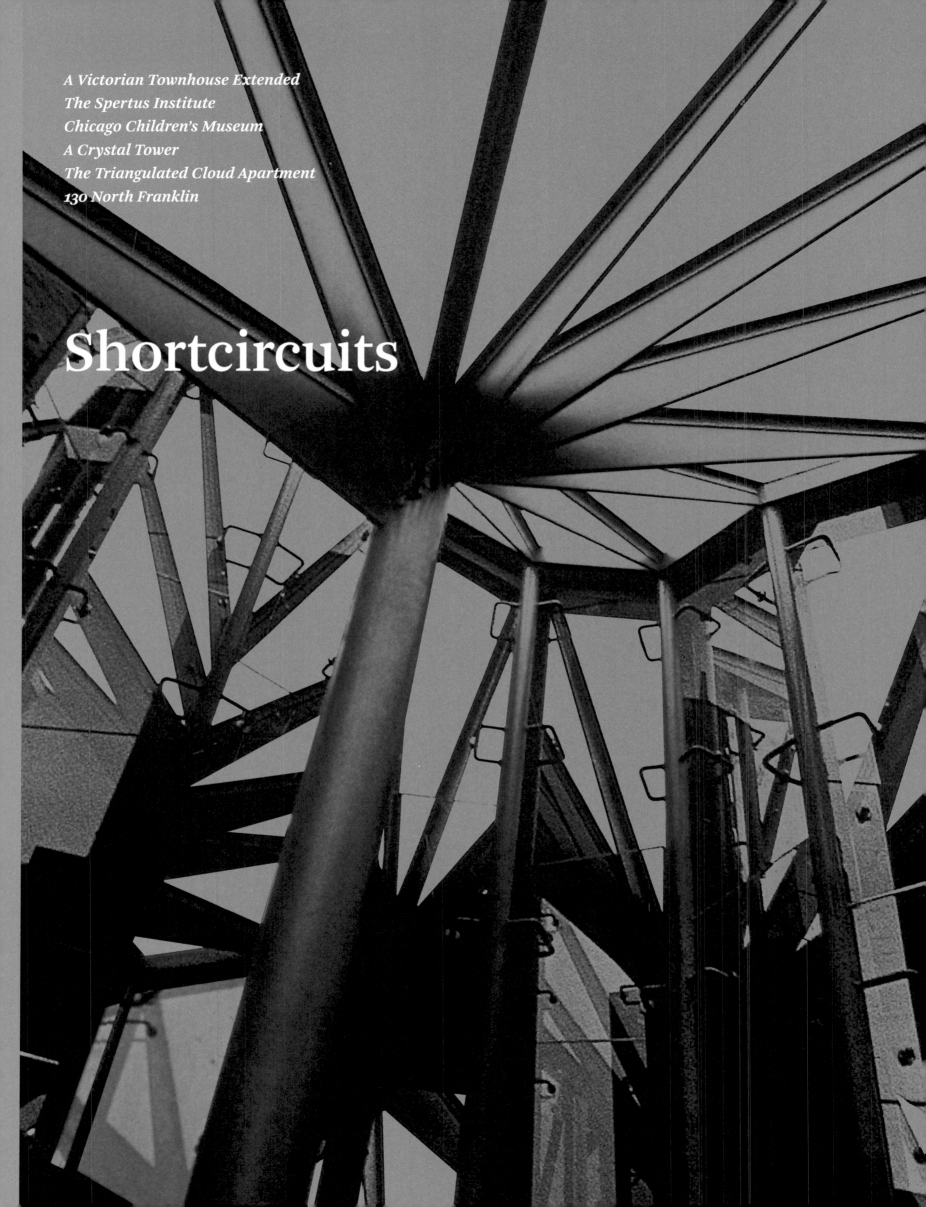

Shortcircuits

THE FIRST APPEARANCE of facets in our work was a reaction to specific project demands. We were completing interior renovations for A Victorian Townhouse Extended when the client decided to expand the house toward the garden. Within the house, we had responded to the confined spaces and period detailing, including decorative moldings, with curvilinear moves that introduced contemporary spaces for the family. The extension, however, permitted freer layouts without stylistic restriction. We concentrated on capturing available daylight and directing it into the house, producing a glassy crystalline structure with bays at different angles, which generated multiple reflections, and ceilings of glass block, which offered a continuous luminosity.

Much of the addition is contained between aluminum-clad four-story walls and canopies that shelter the open terraces and direct views from the interiors. To release the apparent weight, we tapered the aluminum to narrow edges that form aircraft-like wings. Light steel members, sheathed in clear, tinted, and mirrored glass, frame the complex configuration of spaces. But it was a spiral stair that prompted the most thoroughly faceted construction. The tinted mirrored glass that encloses the steel and glass stair takes the shape of a polygon inflected and distorted by the pressures from neighboring walls and adjacent volumes. This extension rises to a translucent roof, fanlike in shape, composed of triangular glass facets. Overall, the arrangement of many-sided interior spaces and folded volumes was, in a sense, a venture into a baroque world. It was not just an extension of a townhouse but an extension of the modernist vocabulary.

Angular geometries also characterized our first large-scale urban building, though a faceted solution did not immediately come to mind. The Spertus Institute for Jewish Learning and Leadership presented both an extraordinary opportunity and a challenging setting. The site was the only vacant lot in the Michigan Boulevard Historic District, the "wall" of traditional facades (by noted architects including Louis Sullivan, Daniel Burnham, and Holabird & Roche) facing Grant Park and Lake Michigan.

Our early studies incorporated a palette of stone, metal, and glass, materials similar to those of the neighboring buildings; we thought the selection also captured something of the institute's program of study of a five-thousand-year-old culture. But we quickly realized that this conventional solution to context was contrary to the spirit of the earlier structures, which had pushed the building technology of their times. We began to consider cutting-edge construction systems and at the same time examined the context more closely. Even though the historic row is referred to as a "wall," it is anything but flat, with surface breaks, modulations, and shifts that complement its perceived unity.

It was something of a breakthrough when we saw the potentials inherent in a single material of our own day: glass. We composed a front with triangular areas of glazing that subtly shift in and out as they respond to internal energies and external pressures. At street level, we lifted and flared this envelope a bit—like a politely raised skirt—to form a sheltered entrance and establish a base for the faceted composition as a whole. At the top, the glass front culminates in an irregular cornice (unlike the classic base-shaft-top formulations of nearby buildings), another nod to the open-ended learning advanced by Spertus. The facade, consisting of 39 triangular planes and 726 pieces of glass cut in 556 shapes, could not have been produced without computer support. A custom Y-shaped mullion accommodates the frames of the glass wall at various angles.

The continuous membrane of glass allowed us to admit the maximum amount of daylight and provide extended views of the park and lakefront. Inside, large atriums at the ground floor and top of the building draw daylight deep into the volume. At the roof, a skylight disperses natural illumination down four floors, brightening the gallery and library below. A floating auditorium playfully reflects light off its faceted plaster form.

We were to some extent surprised but mainly gratified that the facade won support from the city commission that reviews designs for this landmark district. The approval confirmed that the building reinforced the integrity of the "wall" without imitating it. The city allowed the faceted front to project seven feet over the sidewalk in a number of places—the same distance as a balcony on Adler & Sullivan's nearby Auditorium Building. The extensions corresponded to key interior spaces, offering Spertus staff and visitors views north and south along Michigan Avenue. Precise proportion and scale of the facade enabled our visions and technologies to become part of the history of the avenue, which after all is not a fixed moment but a continuum.

The Chicago Children's Museum was another project where a sequence of decisions, in this case relating to what was permitted within Grant Park, generated an assemblage of facets. Located at the north end of the park along Randolph Street, on a site that drops seventeen feet between street and park, and across from several recent residential high-rises, the design had to preserve unobstructed park views for residents.

Initially we developed a street-level lobby. But at a certain point the guidelines shifted to maintain street-level—not just upper-level—views, and we were therefore required to fit the entire museum below the street. The solution we devised incorporated as much south-facing glass as possible to introduce adequate daylight to the interiors. As the museum stepped down a series of sloped ground planes, triangulated glass united the architecture with ramps and planted rooftops, providing an accessible path linking city and park, a rich civic experience not contemplated in the museum's program. Our proposal called to mind the cut surfaces of Lucio Fontana's paintings, which exposed the magical spaces beyond. Here, however, the interlocking interior and exterior constituted both a building and a landscape. At the same time, the glass facets embedded in the green park produced an inherently playful prospect, extending an invitation for children to come, to learn, and to play.

Our conceptual project for *Architectural Record*'s Millennium Issue, A Crystal Tower, was inspired by Mies's glass tower studies of 1919–21, buildings envisioned with folded walls of clear glass. Contextually, however, it responded to its prominent site—a triangle where key thoroughfares converge at the south side of the Chicago River, facing the iconic Tribune Tower and Wrigley Building. We believe that future towers will have to encourage street-level activity by offering openness and a design vocabulary focused on the pedestrian. It will be important to give back to the city with open community spaces. The skyscraper's public role was especially relevant here given the central location of the site and its unique deviation from the Chicago grid.

At the base we proposed a circular bowl, open to pedestrians; the structure and services for the tower are placed at the margins. The vertical volumes, defined by tautly interlocked folded glass surfaces, take on a distinctive buoyancy and hover above the bowl. The floating forms are supported by exoskeletons that allow them to morph as they rise from sleek curves to folded surfaces of glass. A glowing golden beacon crowns this attenuated composition.

Looking back, we have come to think of our interiors as cinematic worlds, designed to be controlled and developed in all dimensions. Experiencing them is like going to the movies: it is not until moviegoers exit the theater that they realize they were magically transported to another world. The plan for The Triangulated Cloud Apartment is in part a response to the geometry of Chicago's One Magnificent Mile, a 1980s apartment complex of extruded polygonal towers. The triangulated forms of the towers reverberate throughout the residence. Our client asked for a porous open plan for living that would take advantage of the boundless views. The bedrooms are the only private spaces; functional areas are integrated within the open layout and work around structural elements and mechanical risers. These interruptions set fixed points that helped to choreograph new functional components of varying heights. The spaces between the components became pathways. The three-sided geometries of the building turned inward to develop a language for the space in which no edge was neglected.

The ceiling extended the same aesthetic with triangulated planes that mediate and integrate the continuous shifts of the internal space delineators. Illuminated edges within the ceilings and spaces between the planes reinforce the circulation pathways. A limited palette of pale colors gives rise to a cloudlike atmosphere. The wood cabinetry and sharp edges of the functional insertions punctuate and counter the cloud as they slice through the space, generating an ambiguity that does not allow conceptually distinct spaces to exist.

Our largest project in Chicago is a study for 130 North Franklin, an office building in Chicago's West Loop. At forty-eight stories, it towers above the surrounding buildings. We worked on the exterior and interior simultaneously, considering preliminary design options for the facade at the same time as we refined the core and internal functions. The solutions ranged from restrained rectangles to fluid curves to multiple geometries.

The client selected an articulated facade, designed for optimum envelope performance. It admits an abundance of daylight and liberates views from the familiar parallel and perpendicular perspectives, providing a unique opportunity for tenants to experience the urban fabric. On the primary, east and west facades, the facets are stretched, while on the north and south, they are gently folded. The aligned building fronts of the adjacent blocks frame and reinforce two plazas that we established on Franklin Street, detaching our building from its context and allowing it to stand alone. Because of this siting, our tower reads as an object: its proportions and the scale of its facets had to be perfectly harmonized. These complex configurations helped to break down the mass but at the same time didn't allow for extreme movements. Our rigorous studies resulted in a clear and tautly controlled composition where no move feels extraneous. We used the freedoms found in this project to enhance the plazas. The open spaces became the street-level focus of the project; as points of punctuation within the urban grid, they return to the city a much-needed openness and release pedestrians from the otherwise straight pathways and vistas, just as the facets above release views from rectilinear visual prospects.

A Victorian Townhouse Extended

Chicago, Illinois, 1985

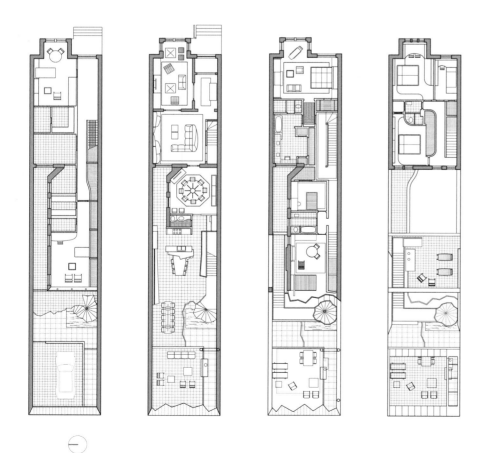

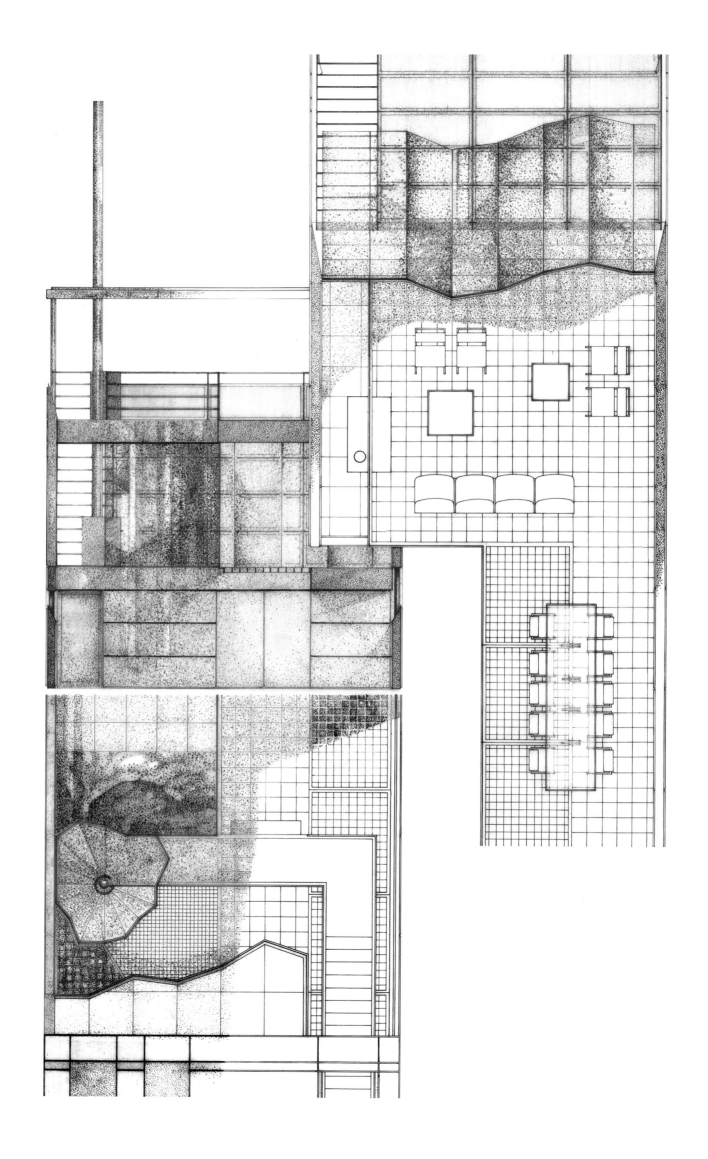

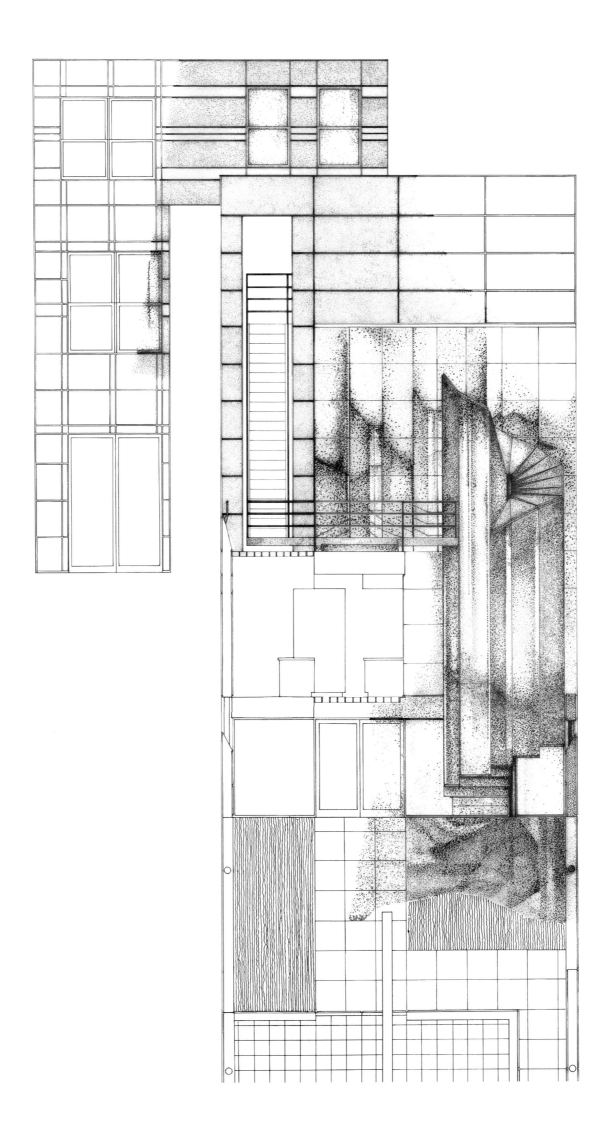

The Spertus Institute

Chicago, Illinois, 2007

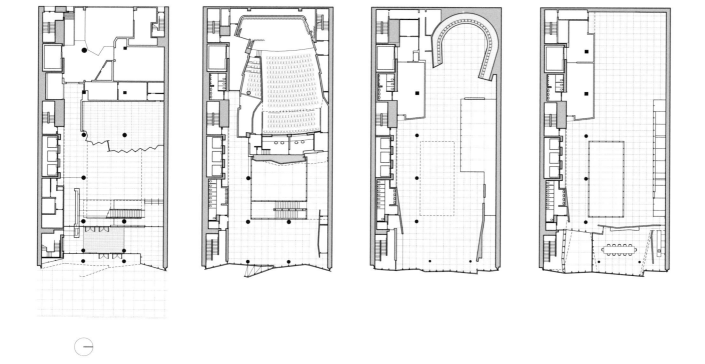

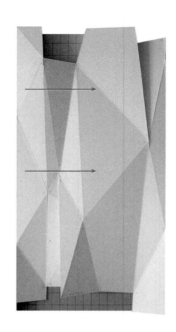

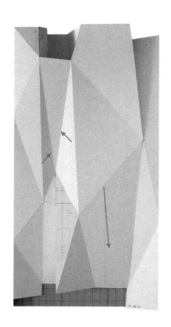

Chicago Children's Museum

Chicago, Illinois, 2008

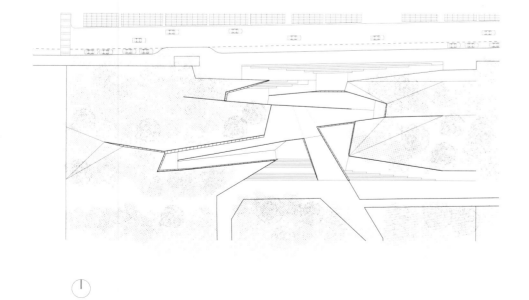

A Crystal Tower

Chicago, Illinois, 1999

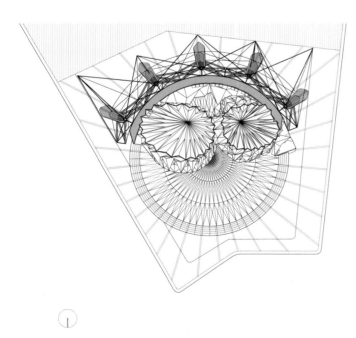

1

The Triangulated Cloud Apartment

Chicago, Illinois, 2012

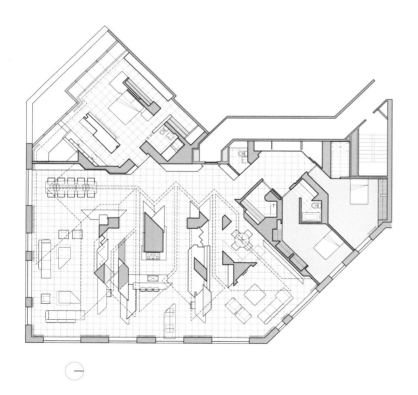

130 North Franklin

Chicago, Illinois, 2012

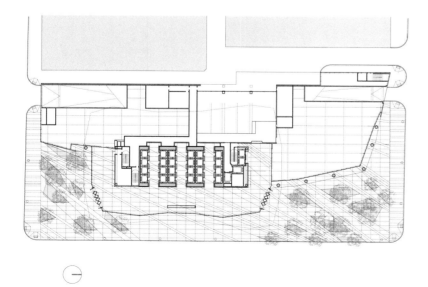

Combines

AS OUR WORK EVOLVES, the freedoms we have uncovered have amplified the geometries—rectangular, curved, and faceted. Each has supplied its own flexibilities, restrictions, and resolutions. Rigorously applied, these geometries foster further, richer configurations of space. Additionally, they may be integrated, a practice that produces new interpretations.

The first executed design that juxtaposed our previous geometries was the flagship showroom for Herman Miller in Chicago's Merchandise Mart. The client wanted to bring a new energy to the showroom, to have a space that would look impressive whether empty or exploding with product. We juxtaposed grids, curves, and facets to offer new design potentials. In some cases, we elaborated and took into another dimension moves that had been implied in previous projects.

We rendered and detailed glass in a variety of ways in response to the program and internal organization, and also to create an abstraction of the preexisting container of the showroom. Fractured glass across the front of the reception area returns some space to the corridor, resulting in an unexpected synchronization and extending a welcome to visitors. A shingled configuration of glass bends and bows around the contours of the conference rooms and simultaneously activates the entry. Freely pivoting glass—a vertical venetian blind—in front of the existing punched windows promotes a staccato reading around the perimeter.

The showroom serves as an all-white stage set, easily adaptable to changing displays. Theatrical lighting allows for color changes while spotlighting the products. The example of Charles and Ray Eames prompted us to concentrate on common materials, exploring their potential by detailing them appropriately. An egg-crate ceiling of painted particleboard modulates to accommodate the existing mechanical systems and soars to achieve the highest possible ceiling heights in the exhibition areas. The billowing surface provides continuous movement, compressing and then releasing forces to energize a space that would have otherwise seemed oppressive. Computer-controlled fabrication integrated the ceiling components, each different, into the overall system.

The two Transparent Houses introduced us to a new world of sand and water: a barrier island off Florida's Gulf Coast. The terrain called for structures that sat lightly on the land, since local building regulations required buildings to be a minimum of twelve feet above storm surge tides.

Transparent House No 1 was designed as an extension of the white sand dunes of the area. At one end, it would have been grounded in the land; at the other, it would have hovered above the sand. The main volume of the house was an elevated, irregularly curving linear volume—a wavelike form that responded to the shoreline and the dunes. The supporting structure consisted of tapered concrete piers in a meandering line; floor slabs were cantilevered on either side. Steel frames springing from the edges of the floor slabs would have bowed out and back as they rose, supporting an envelope of clear glass. On the short ends of the structure, horizontal floor planes extended beyond these glass sails to provide elevated terraces. A circle inscribed in the ground anchored and centered the house and the site, incorporating automobile access, terrace areas, and a pool bounded by two intersecting arcs. Rooftop terraces were shaded by broad canopies with triangulated frames; within the frames photovoltaic cells were embedded in laminated glass.

As we developed the design for this house, the client unexpectedly shifted the site. He had acquired the tip of the island, which he had long been seeking. Close as the properties were physically, the second tract presented very different design conditions.

The site for Transparent House № 2, unlike the linear plot of the first house, offered a wide sweep of panoramic views, suggesting a plan based on an arc. The concrete piers we had devised for the original house would have blocked the views for arriving guests, so we designed a structure that supports the volume of the house on arrays of stainless-steel tubes rising at angles—"sprouts"—which frame the view appealingly.

A series of continuous travertine-paved planes shifts up and down to form the main entrance, pool deck, and open and covered terraces. A curving wall of clear glass on the water side and a straight wall of glazed and metal panels on the approach side enclose the two-story residential volume. The metal panels crimp and fold in reaction to the compression put forth by the house's dominant curvature. The living spaces within are composed of open areas on the main level, mezzanine-like spaces on the upper level, and softly curved enclosures throughout.

A guest pavilion anchors one end of the residence. The disruption between pavilion and main house is expressed by a tear that allows stairs and porches to project outside the principal volume. The exposed torn edges, freed of the overriding geometries, are defined by fast and slow curves and occasional sharp folds of glass and steel. These complexities bring the real and phenomenal components of the house into resolution in the dominant curve drawn from the unique triangular site.

Our entry to the invited competition for an expansion of the Amerika-Gedenkbibliothek (American Library in Berlin) derived from the complexities of the urban site, the historic symbolism of the institution, and the demands of the program. By no means least among the requirements was that the subtly curved multistory block of the original library—a gift from the United States to the people of Berlin during the Cold War—was not to be visually compromised.

We accepted the high-rise slab of the existing building, designed by a group of German modernists led by Fritz Bornemann, as a found object and collaged it with the new components of the library in much the same way that Robert Rauschenberg incorporated found objects into his Combines. The long, gridded arc of the original structure would remain the prominent terminus to Friedrichstrasse. Our addition, expanding to the northeast, was raised to permit freer circulation to a historic park beyond and at the same time to institute an effective interaction with neighboring buildings.

A new entrance to the open ground-floor space provides access to an auditorium, remodeled children's library, and exhibition spaces in a multistory volume. A stair rises around a central node. As this stair spirals, it is as if centrifugal forces have taken control, spinning off circular stairs of smaller radii to reach the upper floors. The center of this baroque development occurs at the intersection of two major internal axes established by the existing building and the addition.

Crystalline envelopes enclose the ramps that connect the floors of the original library to those of the new structure. Curved wings of perforated aluminum scoop the space of the Friedrichstrasse plaza into the library, continuing the dialogue between old and new and at the same time modulating and quieting the views from within. These extended wings are one of the most important components of the project, integrating the rich complexity of forms and varying axes that run through the site. The composition prevents reading the building as an object, instead transforming it into part of the broader urban canvas.

Key components of A Federal Office Building, located in South Florida, were 375,000 square feet of offices, parking for 500 automobiles, heightened security, the unique landscape of the Everglades— and light. Our primary design objective was to foster connections—among the building, its occupants, and the surrounding environment. Sitting on the edge of Everglades National Park, the building embraces restored wetlands. Its chameleon-like surface changes appearance during the course of each day as it reflects the fluctuating hues of its surroundings and the constantly adjusting light of sky and clouds.

Providing comfort for the employees—while respecting both security and freedom of movement— was another important design influence. We divided the bulk of the office space into two towers and made each of them narrow enough to provide natural light and views for all. The central link between the towers defines two courtyards: one at the east, with more formal planting and a reflecting pool, which serves as the entry; one at the west, less formal and open to the wetlands, which is accessible only to employees.

Separating the building into two towers was like splitting an agate in half: it triggered formal reverberations throughout the project. The central link and the courtyard-facing walls took on faceted shapes, as if reacting to that critical fracture. The outer walls of the towers, on the other hand, remain subtle and sinuous warped planes. Inside, the axes of the office floors shift along with the curvature, yielding for viewers continuously changing angles.

Exterior envelopes consist of specially treated thermal glass that minimizes heat gain and glare while admitting enough daylight to make artificial lighting mostly unnecessary. Perforated-metal solar shades support environmental sustainability, blocking and reflecting light without obstructing views. This largest-scale realization of the integration of our characteristic geometries resulted from our determination to emphasize a fundamental design objective—the connection that permeated every aspect of the program. As we look back, we realize that this synthesis was possible only owing to our previous investigations of rectangles, curves, and facets.

A Herman Miller Showroom

Chicago, Illinois, 2001

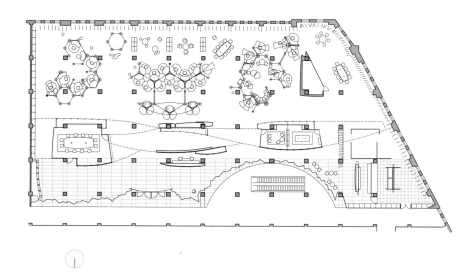

Transparent House № 1

Gulf Coast, Florida, 1999

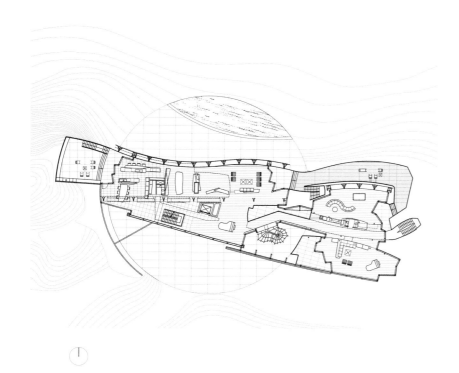

Transparent House № 2

Gulf Coast, Florida, 2005

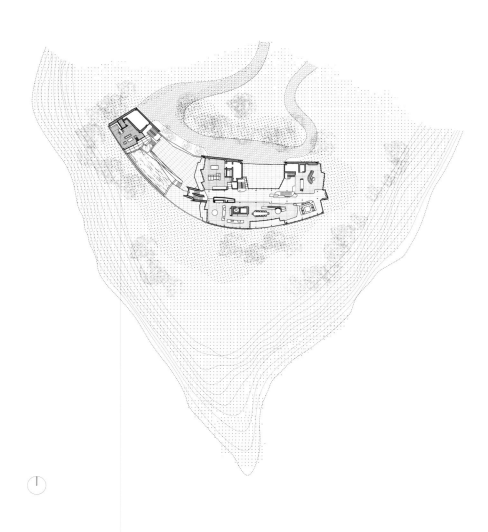

Amerika-Gedenkbibliothek
(American Library in Berlin)

Berlin, Germany, 1988

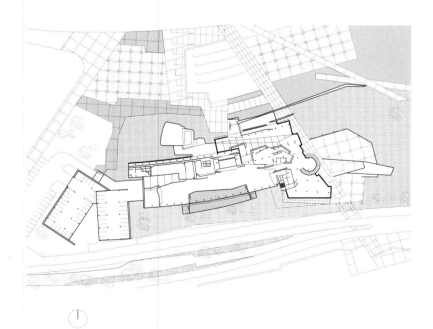

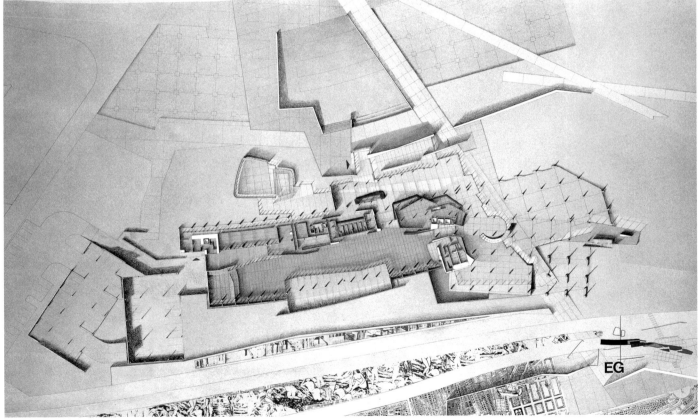

A Federal Office Building

Miramar, Florida, 2014

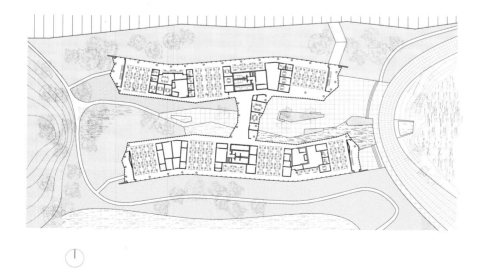

Chronology of Works

1981 A Steel and Glass House 1982 The Thonet Showroom 1983 The Painted Apartment / Dart Gallery / Joseph Cornell Galleries, Art Institute of Chicago 1984 Hartmarx Corporate Offices 1985 A Victorian Townhouse Extended / RK Chaise / The Chicago Chair 1986 Stone Residence / Untitled № 3 / Bannockburn Lake Office Plaza (Bannockburn, IL) / Schal Associates Corporate Offices 1987 Untitled № 1 1988 Untitled № 2 / Untitled № 4 / Amerika-Gedenkbibliothek (American Library in Berlin, Germany) / Hewitt Associates Corporate Headquarters (Lincolnshire, IL) / Frank C. Nasher Advertising Offices 1989 Hewitt Associates Eastern Regional Center (Rowayton, CT) / Chemical Bank Offices / Dow Jones Telerate Office

1990 Marketing Corporation of America, Lee Hill Corporation Offices 1992 The Stainless Steel Apartment / Cloud Apartment № 1 / Northern Trust Company, Investment Center (Toronto, ONT, Canada) 1993 Northern Trust Company of California, Bank and Corporate Offices (Los Angeles, CA) / Silverman Residence 1994 Hart Schaffner and Marx Factory Consolidation / Northern Trust Company of California (Newport Beach, CA) 1995 The Arts Club of Chicago / William Switzer and Associates Showrooms 1996 A Brick and Glass House / Arian, Lowe and Travis Offices / Western Textile Corporate Office (Deerfield, IL) 1997 Jyvaskyla Music and Arts Center (Jyvaskyla, Finland) / IDEO Offices (Evanston, IL) / World Savings (Palatine, IL) 1998 A Herman Miller Showroom, Phase 1 / Christie's Showroom and Offices / Museum of Science and Industry, Rotunda Study 1999 Transparent House № 1 (Gulf Coast, FL) / A Crystal Tower (*Architectural Record*, Millennium Issue)

Unless stated otherwise, all projects are located in Chicago, IL.

For projects completed prior to 1991, the architect of record is Krueck & Olsen Architects.

2000 Museum of Contemporary Art Improvements / Urban Furniture / Christie's Showroom and Offices (Coral Gables, FL) / Pullman Bank 2001 Phillips Plastics Molding Facility (Phillips, WI) / Herman Miller C1 Renovation, Main Site (Zeeland, MI) / A Herman Miller Showroom, Phase 2 / Herman Miller National Design Center (Los Angeles, CA) / Chicago Architecture Foundation / Dormitory, Illinois Institute of Technology 2003 Allianz Insurance Company Offices / Herman Miller National Design Center (Washington, DC) / Lucien Rollin Showroom 2004 Crown Fountain / Shure Incorporated, Technology Annex (Niles, IL) 2005 S. R. Crown Hall Restoration / Hafen City, Chicago Square (Hamburg, Germany) / Herman Miller National Design Center (Dallas, TX) / Herman Miller National Design Center (New York, NY) / 600 South Wabash Studios / Transparent House № 2 (Gulf Coast, FL) 2006 Chicago Christian Industrial League, Roosevelt Road Campus / Herman Miller National Design Center (Atlanta, GA) / Hubbard Street Dance Chicago / Project Orient (Tbilisi, Georgia) 2007 The Spertus Institute / Muntu Dance Theater Chicago / H113 Residential Master Plan (Chennai, India) / Chicago Mercantile Exchange, Facade and Lobby Renovation / Gordon Residence / Playa Vista, Parcel 1 (Los Angeles, CA) 2008 Chicago Children's Museum, Daley Bicentennial Plaza / School of Social Service Administration Restoration, University of Chicago / Museum of Science and Industry, Space Exhibit Study 2009 Dwight D. Eisenhower Memorial (Washington, DC) / 11730 Pennsylvania Avenue Facade (Washington, DC) / 860–880 Lake Shore Drive Apartments Restoration / 1100 First Street (Washington, DC) / Abrahamic Interfaith Center / Shure Incorporated, S. N. Shure Theater (Niles, IL) / Cloud Apartment № 2 (Milwaukee, WI)

2010 Rouse Headquarters Historic Preservation Guidelines (Columbia, MD) 2012 Lake Point Tower Study / The Triangulated Cloud Apartment / 130 North Franklin Office Tower / Reston Crossing Master Plan (Reston, VA) / Farnsworth House Restoration and Study (Plano, IL) / 1150 First Street (Washington, DC) / Edward H. Levi Administration Building Portal, University of Chicago / Chicago Children's Museum, Navy Pier / Federal Center Post Office, Feasibility Study 2013 Pacific Island Embassy Campus, Port Moresby, Papua New Guinea 2014 College of Medicine Learning Center, University of Illinois at Chicago / Fermi Lab CDF-XOC (Batavia, IL) / Schatz Event Space / A Federal Office Building (Benjamin P. Grogan and Jerry L. Dove FBI Building, Miramar, FL) 2016 Shure Incorporated, Great Hall (Niles, IL) / United Airlines LAX International Terminal Expansion (Los Angeles, CA) / 222 Hudson Boulevard Office Tower (New York, NY) / The Franklin Lobby 2017 Barack Obama Foundation Flex Space / 190 South LaSalle Lobby / 10 and 30 South Wacker Lobby / Reston Crossing Master Plan, Schematic Design (Reston, VA)

Krueck + Sexton Architects
1981–2017

Ronald A. Krueck
FAIA

Ron, founding partner, received his BArch from the College of Architecture at the Illinois Institute of Technology and also studied painting at the School of the Art Institute of Chicago.

In 1983 Ron was named an "emerging voice" by the Architectural League of New York; in 1986 he was recognized as one of "40 Under 40" top architects in the United States by *Interiors* magazine; and in 1993 he was inducted into the Interior Design Hall of Fame. He was made a Fellow of the American Institute of Architects in 1992 and received the Lifetime Achievement Award from the Chicago AIA in 2016.

Ron taught design as a studio professor at the Illinois Institute of Technology for thirty years. He has also been a visiting professor at the Harvard Graduate School of Design.

An advocate for the preservation of modern architecture, Ron is a founding member of the Friends of the Farnsworth House and the Mies van der Rohe Society. He served on the Board of Trustees for Fallingwater for ten years and is a member of the Committee of 20th Century and Contemporary Art at the Art Institute of Chicago.

Mark P. Sexton
FAIA, LEED AP

Mark, founding partner, received his BArch from the College of Architecture at the Illinois Institute of Technology and currently serves on its Board of Advisors. He is a member of the National Registry of Peer Professionals of the GSA Design Excellence Program and the Advisory Design Council of the School of the Art Institute of Chicago and is on the faculty of the McCormick School of Engineering at Northwestern University.

Mark was recognized as a Fellow of the American Institute of Architects in 2006 and participates in the Bridge mentor program sponsored by AIA Chicago, the College of Fellows, and the Young Architects Forum. He lectures at universities, cultural institutions, and conferences worldwide and participates on national design juries.

He sits on the Building and Grounds Committees of St. Clement Church and the Pattington Condominium Association, advising on the historical integrity of these more-than-hundred-year-old buildings.

We are grateful to the talented individuals who have worked in our offices. Their efforts have made possible the buildings and projects shown in this book: Katherine Bajor / Brett Bowers / Antonio Caliz / Bill Callahan / John Carhart / Russell Castle / Nicolas Caulliez / Frank Cavanaugh / Rico Cedro / Yugene Cha / Chun Cham / Jamie Cook / Carolyn Corogan / Martin Dahl / Jesper Dalskov / Paul Danna / Ursula Dayenian / John DeKraker / Tod Desmarias / Edward Donnely / Rich Drozd / Jake Eble / John Ekholm / Mircea Eni / Maria Escudero / Rob Falconer / Laura Fehlberg / Jason Fisher / Callie Fleetwood / Ian Ford / Rachael Frank / Faron Franks / Bryan Frey / Mark Frey / Richard Gnat / Ricardo Gonzalez / Fred Grier / Luke Haas / Chris Hanke / Katie Hart / Christina Henning / Hyunjin Im / John Janda / Perry Janke / Peter Johannknecht / Drew Johnson / Matthew Johnson / Robin Johnson / Amy Jordan / Jongyoun Jung / Werner Karl / Shin Kim / Parus Kiravanich / Winston Koh /

Thomas Jacobs
FAIA, LEED BD+C

Tom joined Krueck + Sexton Architects in 1997 and was made a partner in 2011. He received his MS in Architecture from the Swiss Federal Institute of Technology ETH in Zurich, Switzerland.

Tom worked at Herzog & de Meuron, where he was a member of the design team for the new de Young Museum in San Francisco. He is an adjunct associate professor at the Illinois Institute of Technology and has taught graduate and undergraduate design studios as well as the seminar "Good Business Is Good Design."

Tom embraces the role of "citizen architect," promoting healthy and livable communities, and in 2016 co-founded Architects Advocate: Action on Climate Change, a nonpartisan, grass-roots network of architecture firms nationwide. He has lectured at academic institutions, architectural conventions, and civic organizations, integrating his experiences as a practicing architect, teacher, and advocate.

Scott Pratt
FAIA, LEED AP

Scott joined Krueck + Sexton Architects in 2010 as associate principal and was made a partner in 2015. He received his BArch from the College of Architecture at the Illinois Institute of Technology; during that time, he worked as an intern with C. F. Murphy Associates under Gene Summers and Helmut Jahn.

After he graduated, Scott served in the U.S. Navy Construction Battalions in a construction management role on Diego Garcia, British Indian Ocean Territory. He then spent three decades at Murphy/Jahn. As principal architect he executed the design of more than twenty buildings, including the University of Chicago's Mansueto Library; Liberty Place Towers in Center City Philadelphia; Hyatt Regency in Roissy, France; Filmhaus Museum at Sony Center Berlin; and Schiff Residences, Chicago.

Scott is a member of the Lean Construction Institute and the Society for College and University Planning and serves on the Leadership Council of Chicago's historic Moody Church.

Paul Kozlowski / Kit Krankel / Craig Krupitzer / Keith Lasko / Heidi Lee / James Lewis / Miles Lindblad / Melissa Lockwood / Eli Logan / Luis Lopez / Sara Lundgren / Ruijie Ma / Kathleen Maciejko / Oliver Mack / William Mahalko / Andrea Mason / Lucinda Mellott / Jozef Mierwa / Chungho Min / Jacek Mrligala / Fred Norris / Ryan Ornberg / Hans Papke / Brandson Pass / Chirag Patel / Chris Phillips / Robert Piotrowski / Lauren Raab / Vladimir Radutny / Drew Ranieri / Bill Rich / Jason Roberts / Michael Robinson / John Ronan / Norberto Rosenstein / Eric Schall / Greg Schmidt / Patricia Schroetner / Andrea Schwappach / Don Semple / Thomas Shafer / Alex Sims / Jennifer Stanovich / Jeremy Stanulis / Susan Stevens / Phil Stott / Kevin Taylor / Paul Tebben / Lindsey Telford / Marvin Thomas / Hans Thummel / Jaquelin Tijerina / Timothy Tracey / Brendan Tucker / Juan Villafane / Daniel Waas / Annie Wang / Jake Watkins / Ulrik Weinert / Don Wetzel / Edward Witkowski / Zhouli Xie / David Zawko / James Zeigler

We acknowledge the dedication and efforts of the book team. This publication would not have been possible without them:

Rutger Fuchs, graphic designer,
  Rutger Fuchs Amsterdam
Patrick Goley, prepress and color manager,
  Professional Graphics Inc.
Sara Lundgren, K+S project director,
  Krueck + Sexton Architects
Andrea Monfried, commissioning editor,
  The Images Publishing Group

We appreciate the many photographers who have documented our work for almost forty years:

Richard Bryant: 88, 94, 121, 123, 125
Cheri Eisenberg: 164
Yukio Futagawa/GA Photographers: 96, 117, 118–19, 120
Steve Hall/Hedrich Blessing: 15, 19, 67, 68–69, 70, 71, 74, 75, 76, 77, 79, 81, 82, 84, 85, 86–87, 148, 183, 184–85, 187, 188, 189, 204, 210, 211
Bill Hedrich/Hedrich Blessing: 10, 16, 21, 22–23
Jim Hedrich/Hedrich Blessing: 124
Wolfgang Hoyt/ESTO: 93, 100–101, 103 upper left, 104 middle, 105
Timothy Hursley: 18, 25, 30–31, 99, 103 upper right, 103 lower left, 103 lower right, 106–7, 127
ImageFiction: 191, 192–93, 196–97
Barbara Karant/Abbey Sadin: 24
Krueck + Sexton Architects: 83, 135, 137, 138, 139, 140, 158, 171, 172, 173, 174–75, 177, 179, 180, 181, 194, 195, 218
Krueck + Sexton Architects/collection of Art Institute of Chicago: 26–27, 34, 102, 110, 151, 152–53, 154–55
Krueck + Sexton Architects/photographed by Hedrich Blessing: 42, 244, 245, 247
Marco Lorenzetti/Hedrich Blessing: 17, 41, 43, 44, 45, 47, 48–49, 51, 52, 53, 54, 55, 56, 57, 144, 209, 212, 213, 243, 248–49
Kendall McCaugherty/Hedrich Blessing: 147
Nick Merrick/Hedrich Blessing: 14, 33, 35, 36, 37, 38–39, 95, 97, 104 left, 104 right, 109, 111, 112, 113, 114–15, 128–29, 130, 131, 132, 133, 198, 205, 207, 251, 252–53, 254, 255, 256–57, 258, 259, 260, 261, 263, 264–65
Millennium Park Inc.: 80
Mariusz Mizera: 59, 60, 61, 62, 63, 64–65, 92, 202, 214, 215, 217, 219, 220, 221, 222–23, 228, 229, 230, 231, 232, 233, 234, 235
Phillip Turner: 28–29
Paul Warchol: 46
William Zbaren: 72, 73, 145, 146, 149, 157, 159, 160, 161, 162–63, 165, 167, 168–69, 203, 206, 225, 226–27, 236, 237, 238–39, 240–41, 268, 269

Published in Australia in 2017 by
The Images Publishing Group Pty Ltd
ABN 89 059 734 431
6 Bastow Place, Mulgrave, Victoria 3170, Australia
Tel: +61 3 9561 5544 Fax: +61 3 9561 4860
books@imagespublishing.com
www.imagespublishing.com

Copyright © Krueck + Sexton Architects 2017
The Images Publishing Group Reference Number: 1389

National Library of Australia Cataloguing-in-Publication entry:

Title: Krueck + Sexton : from there to here.

ISBN: 9781864707403 (hardback)

Subjects: Krueck + Sexton Architects.
  Architecture, American—Illinois—Chicago.
  International style (Architecture)—Influence.
  Architecture, Modern—20th century.
  Architecture, Modern—21st century.

Printed on 150gsm Munken Kristall by
GöteborgsTryckeriet, Sweden

IMAGES has included on its website a page for special
notices in relation to this and our other publications.
Please visit www.imagespublishing.com

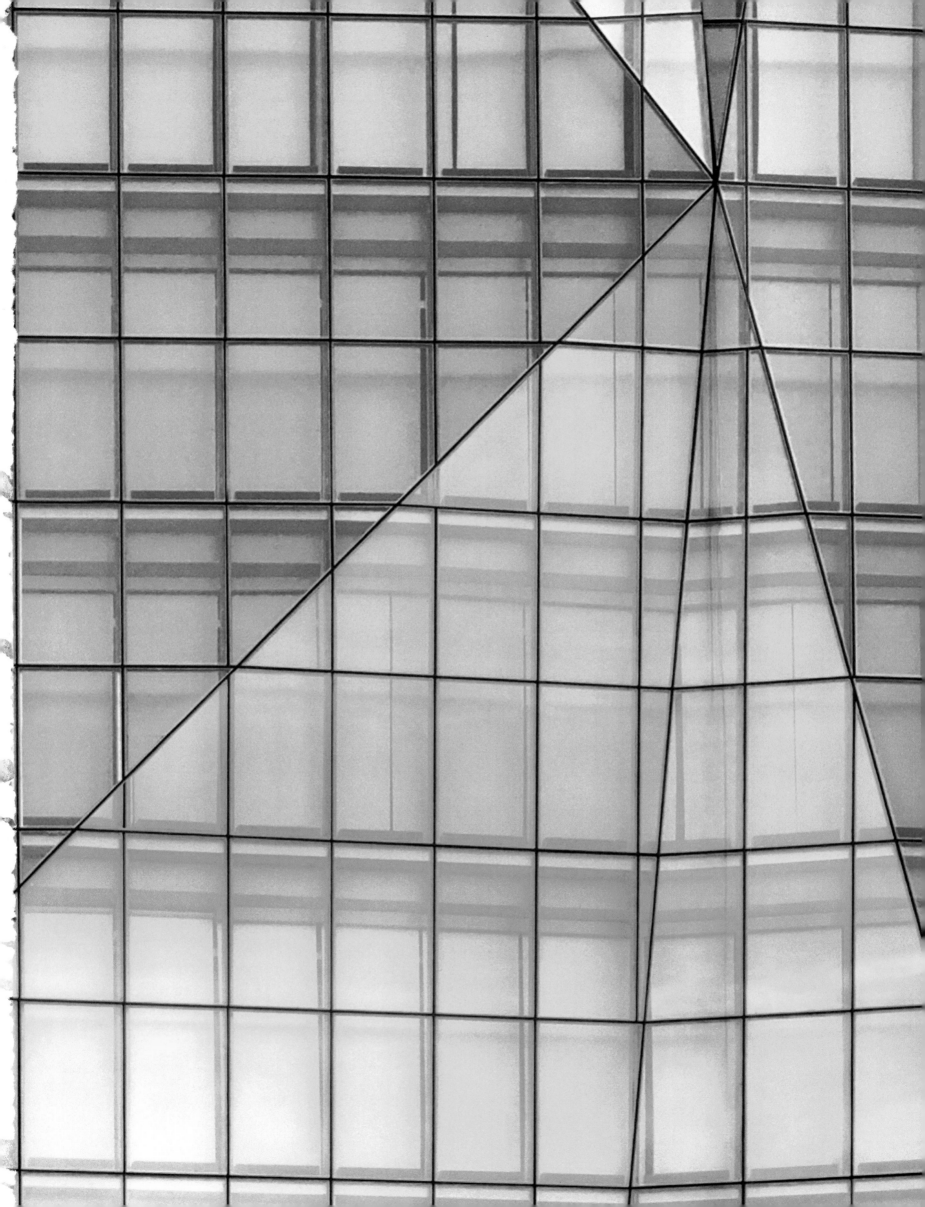